BUSINESS IS PERSONAL

STRATEGIES FOR BUILDING MEANINGFUL RELATIONSHIPS IN BUSINESS AND LIFE

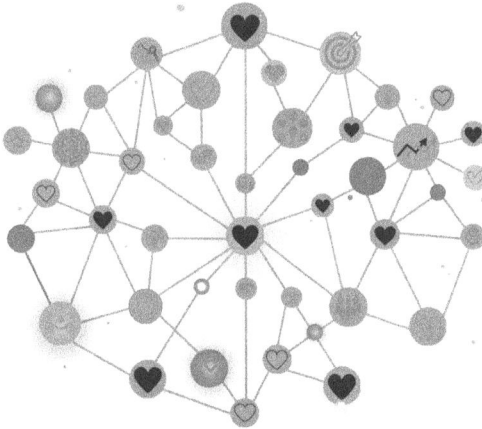

SEAN M. BAIR

BYU ACADEMIC
PUBLISHING

For Dana, Emma, and Seth—
you are my eternal family and my greatest blessing.

And to Chase, Devin, and all the students who contributed their time and talents—your efforts reflect the divine principle that we are all teachers and learners in God's great plan. This book is a shared testament to the knowledge and light we can create when we work together in faith.

CONTENTS

PREFACE

A few years ago, one of the most insightful mentors I had the pleasure of learning from posed a question to our group: What makes a lasting impression? After listening to a variety of thoughtful answers, he offered a perspective that has stayed with me: "Imagine the impact of receiving a personalized message on your birthday from someone in your network. That's the kind of thoughtful gesture that's unforgettable."

This lesson underscored the essence of genuine, authentic, and mindful connections. It's about transcending mere formalities and bridging the gap between the giver and the receiver. In the realm of real connections, the lines blur—we all give, and we all gain.

As I began outlining this book, a key question guided my efforts: "How can I demystify networking, making it accessible and practical for students, entrepreneurs, and professionals alike?"

I've observed the negative connotation often associated with networking. Despite its undeniable power, there's a belief that networking is a self-serving tool primarily aimed at enriching our business or professional lives. This view turns networking into something scary and full of doubt, making us always worry about getting rejected.

But what if we reframe networking as our chance to contribute and connect in the most sincere way possible? This shift in perspective invites a more optimistic and genuine approach to building connections. We start to see success not as the primary goal of networking but as a natural outcome of meaningful engagement. Success, then, becomes a by-product of making our networking efforts truly significant—not just for ourselves, but for everyone we meet.

INTRODUCTION

When we're young, we tend to focus on material possessions as a measure of success. However, as we gain life experience, we come to realize that true fulfillment and happiness come from the four P's: People (the relationships that sustain us), Places (the environments that shape us), Purpose (the driving force behind our actions), and Passion (the spark that ignites our creativity). This book is dedicated to those who are on a journey to pursue their passions, find their purpose, explore new places, and most importantly, build meaningful relationships with others.

In my three decades of experience in the business world, I've come to understand that relationships are the foundation of success. Through my work with major corporations such as Walmart, Target, and Macy's, as well as collaborations with government organizations, universities, and municipalities, I've witnessed firsthand the immense power of building connections.

But networking, also referred to as consociating, isn't just about salesmanship or extroversion. It's about cultivating authentic relationships that empower both parties. And the truth is, businesses and corporations are made up of people. So, if you want to achieve success in both your personal and professional life, it's imperative to prioritize nurturing those relationships.

In this technological age, it's easy to fall into the trap of relying solely on social media platforms like Facebook, Instagram, or LinkedIn to stay in touch with friends and colleagues. However, true networking requires going beyond the superficial, and finding common ground with others, building a foundation of trust, and working towards mutual success.

I've come to realize, albeit embarrassingly late after four decades, that the core principle of networking reflects an age-old wisdom found in the Old Testament: the imperative to love thy neighbor. This connection between ancient wisdom and contemporary networking practices underscores a profound truth: at the core of building effective relationships lies the timeless value of compassion and empathy. It's about seeing our interactions with others not just as transactions, but as opportunities to embody the spiritual values of kindness and mutual respect. By integrating these principles into our networking efforts, we aim to cultivate not only success but also a deeper sense of fulfillment and connection.

Join me on a journey towards becoming a networking pro. Together, we'll delve into essential techniques and tips for building genuine connections that open doors to new opportunities. You might even come to enjoy networking, realizing that success is built on relationships, and there's never a wrong time to start making those connections.

CHAPTER 1

The Business of Becoming Bacon

The Kevin Bacon Game is a popular game that tests one's knowledge of the movie industry (Smith, 2020). The game requires one player to name an actor and another player to find a connection to Kevin Bacon through other actors and movies. For instance, if one says "Kiera Knightly," the other player may mention Donald Sutherland, who played her father in *Pride and Prejudice* and also appeared in *Animal House* with Kevin Bacon. Kiera Knightly is connected to Kevin Bacon through Donald Sutherland in just two degrees of separation. The fun and challenge of the game are found in trying to pick actors unrelated to Kevin Bacon, which is nearly impossible in the movie industry.

In the same manner, business life is like art. There are many "Kevin Bacons" or "Superconnectors" in both business and personal life who seem to know everyone and are well-known by everyone. Your challenge, and my mission for this book, is to make you the Kevin Bacon of business.

The Most Important Skills

According to *The HR Director*, empathy and human connection are now essential skills team members should have in the workplace (Fern, 2014).

Now that our interactions are reduced to endless Zoom meetings and non-stop emails, you must still ignite yourself and your team through empathy and human connection.

Ironically, even though connecting has become easier than ever (we can be in a meeting with someone thousands of miles away from us), the ability to connect more deeply has become a scarce skill.

Due to the greater convenience of connecting online, people forget the skills and courtesy that used to come naturally when communicating with others. There are endless options that we can use now to connect with old friends and create new friendships; some even choose these options over the traditional face-to-face way of meeting with people. But in business, it's different; people still fly in from all over the world just to transact in person.

The ability to establish contacts weighs heavily on one's skills in networking. Many people desire to build relationships but may feel uncomfortable and inadequate. Students and professionals miss many opportunities like work, promotions, and mentorships because they lack the knowledge and skills to network. Most often, those kinds of opportunities are learned from friends and acquaintances. However, not everyone has the desire to grow their network. Nevertheless, it is essential for anyone wanting to advance their professional trajectory.

Contrary to what many believe, the interpersonal skillset including networking, charisma, and making personal connections is not limited to the marketing industry—it can benefit anyone who wants to make giant leaps in life and business.

Why Sending *That* Message Counts

"Some estimate that upwards of 85% of open positions are filled through networking." —*Business Insider*

"80% of available jobs are never advertised." —*Forbes*

"As much as 80% of jobs are filled through personal and professional connections." —*Julia Freeland Fisher, director of education research at the Clayton Christensen Institute*

"85% of respondents found their job via networking" —*Forbes*

Networking is a vital tool in today's world. It enables us to create lasting connections with people that can help us personally and professionally. Suppose you're searching for a new job. Would you rather apply to a company that you know nothing about or a company that you have a connection with? Networking can provide you with opportunities that you may not have found otherwise. As we continue to live in a virtual world, we must master the art of online networking. That's why this book emphasizes the importance of creating meaningful connections that go beyond superficial interactions. By taking the time to get to know someone, you can develop a relationship that will be beneficial for both parties. Networking is an essential aspect of our lives, and it can help us achieve our goals. This book provides practical tips and resources to help you enhance your networking skills and create a lasting impact on those you meet.

CHAPTER 2

Great Networkers

Relationships are hard. But think about it; it's the one thing we all want. To love and be loved. And the one thing that holds us back is just how hard relationships are. —SIMON SINEK

Great networkers do not happen by accident. Similar to how spouses must often make lifestyle changes during the first years of marriage, you have to adapt and develop good networking behaviors before you'll see success in building and maintaining a network. Think of your own social circle. You'll probably be able to pick out a superconnector friend of yours who excels at bringing people together and making them feel at ease. People with this type of magnetic personality are never short of mentors or critical connections. As you learn to draw people in, genuinely listen to who they are and what they care about, and cultivate the relationships you build, you will become a superconnector in your own right.

Becoming an Engaging Person

"To be interesting, be interested." —*Dale Carnegie*

Developing the ability to be interesting and engaging is a valuable skill that can benefit both your personal and professional relationships. By showing genuine interest in others, you can establish meaningful connections and positively influence those around you. Sam Horn's TED talk "The Art of Being Interesting" (Horn, 2016) emphasizes the importance of storytelling in capturing your audience's attention, while Dale Carnegie's classic book "How to Win Friends and Influence People" provides insights on being likable and making a positive impression. Drawing from the wisdom of these networking experts, as well as my own experiences, I've compiled several helpful tips to help you improve your ability to "be interesting."

Step 1: Identify Your Unique Qualities

The first step in becoming interesting is identifying your unique qualities and experiences. These can include personal stories, passions, and interests. Take some time to reflect on what sets you apart from others and what makes you unique. Write down a list of these qualities to help you focus on what you have to offer.

Step 2: Develop Your Storytelling Skills

The next step is to develop your storytelling skills. Sam Horn suggests that we should strive to be storytellers rather than merely telling stories. This means finding a way to make your stories personal, engaging, and memorable. Consider the following tips when developing your storytelling skills:

- Start with a hook that captures your audience's attention.
- Use descriptive language to create vivid images in the mind of your listener.
- Make your story relatable by using humor, emotion, or personal anecdotes.
- Use a clear structure to guide your story from beginning to end.

Step 3: Practice Active Listening

Being interesting also means being a good listener. Dale Carnegie notes that people love to talk about themselves and that showing genuine interest in others is one of the most effective ways to win friends. In order to be an effective listener, practice active listening, which involves giving your full attention, asking questions, and offering genuine feedback.

Step 4: Create a "Be Interesting" Script

The final step is to create a "be interesting" script that you can use in various situations. This script should incorporate the elements of your unique qualities, storytelling skills, and active listening. It should also reflect your personality and style, making it authentic and relatable to those around you. Here is a sample "be interesting" script:

- Start by introducing yourself and sharing a personal story or anecdote that highlights your unique qualities.
- Ask questions to show genuine interest in the person you are talking to.
- Use storytelling to illustrate your points and make your conversation more engaging.
- Listen actively, offering feedback and asking follow-up questions.

The following are a few examples of "be interesting" introductions and elevator pitches from famous individuals.

Steve Jobs: "Good morning! Today, I'm going to introduce you to a revolutionary new product that will change the way we live, work, and communicate. It's called the iPhone, and it's not just a phone, it's a mini computer that fits in your pocket. With the iPhone, you can make calls, send messages, browse the web, take photos, and much more. It's sleek, it's innovative, and it's the future of mobile technology."

Richard Branson: "Hi, I'm Richard Branson, the founder of Virgin Group. I'm an entrepreneur, adventurer, and philanthropist. I believe in the power of innovation, creativity, and pushing the boundaries of what's possible. I'm always looking for new opportunities to make a positive impact on the world, and I'm excited to be here and learn from all of you."

Serena Williams: "Hey everyone, I'm Serena Williams, a professional tennis player and entrepreneur. I'm passionate about sports, fitness, and empowering women to be their best selves. I believe that with hard work, dedication, and a positive mindset, anyone can achieve their goals."

Bill Gates "Hi, I'm Bill Gates, a technology entrepreneur, philanthropist, and co-founder of Microsoft. I am driven by the belief that technology can help us solve some of the world's biggest problems, such as poverty, disease, and climate change. I am convinced that by working collaboratively and utilizing our collective knowledge, we can create a better world for all. I'm excited to meet and learn from everyone here and exchange ideas."

Being interesting is a valuable skill that can help you establish meaningful connections and positively influence those around you. By focusing on your unique qualities, developing your storytelling skills, practicing active listening, and creating a "be interesting" script, you can become an engaging and memorable communicator. Whether it be in personal or professional relationships, being interesting is sure to make a lasting impression.

Listen to Learn and Connect

Beyond becoming an interesting person, you also need to be interested in others. As Bernard Baruch once said, "Most of the successful people I've known are the ones who do more listening than talking." In our modern age, where so much emphasis is placed on being heard, we must remember the value of listening. It's a skill that we can all improve upon, and one that can open doors both personally and professionally.

Listening is the foundation for building strong relationships. When we listen, we gain valuable insights into the thoughts and experiences of others.

This insight allows us to connect with people on a deeper level, regardless of their background or station in life. Whether you're networking for your business or just seeking to build a meaningful connection with someone, listening is an essential skill that you can't afford to overlook.

Respect is one of the most significant values we can show to others, and listening is one of the sincerest forms of respect. It means paying attention not only to the words being spoken but also to non-verbal cues such as posture, facial expressions, and eye contact. By showing that we are listening, we can earn the trust of others and build strong, lasting relationships.

Listening can be used not only to create new relationships but also to improve existing ones. Good communication is vital to most transactions, and poor communication can lead to misunderstandings and conflicts. By truly listening to the needs and desires of others, we can avoid misunderstandings and build stronger, more collaborative relationships.

It's important to note that when we listen, we allow other people to change us. We learn best when we are paying attention. With shared ideas and thoughts, we gain new knowledge and form new opinions. By paying attention to what is being said, we can integrate new insights into our own lives and grow both personally and professionally.

So, if you're looking to improve your networking skills, or just seeking to build more meaningful connections with others, remember the value of listening. By asking the right questions, paying attention to non-verbal cues, and truly understanding the needs and desires of others, you can build stronger relationships and achieve your goals.

Building and Cultivating Relationships for Success

As you balance communicating your own interesting persona with great listening skills and reciprocated interest, you will begin to move past superficial interactions and build a lasting network. It is a crucial aspect of personal and professional development that continues to be important throughout one's career and life. The African proverb "If you want to go fast, go alone. If you want to go far, go with others" holds in this context. Your network of peers, colleagues, and acquaintances plays a vital role in your successes and opportunities.

Networking as an adult may feel different from the collegiate experience, but the principles remain the same: make meaningful connections, build relationships, and always be open to learning and growth.

Here are some tips to help you navigate the world of adult networking:

Resume Upkeep

Keep your resume up to date. Your resume serves as your professional calling card and should always reflect your most current skills and experiences. Regularly update your resume and keep a digital version handy for quick and easy access. This will ensure you are ready to take advantage of opportunities when they arise.

Cultivate Your Network

Cultivate your network. Networking is not a one-and-done task. It is a continuous process of building and nurturing relationships. Stay in touch with your network, participate in events and activities, and actively seek out new connections. Use platforms like LinkedIn to expand your network and stay informed about industry trends and job opportunities.

Serve others. Networking is not just about what others can do for you; it's also about what you can do for others. Seek opportunities to help others, offer advice, and provide support. When you serve others, you build trust and establish yourself as a valuable member of your network. Mentoring is a great way to serve others. Share your time and talents, as well as your trials and tribulations with others so they can learn and grow.

In the spirit of serving and building a network, it's essential to recognize the deeper, more profound unity we share in Christ. Just as Paul writes in Ephesians 4:3, "Make every effort to keep the unity of the Spirit through the bond of peace," our endeavors in networking and serving others are not merely for professional gain but are a reflection of the unity we seek in Christ. This unity transcends professional titles and industry sectors, inviting us into a community where our primary identity is not our profession but our shared faith in Christ.

Embracing this gospel-centered concept of unity in our networking efforts encourages us to look beyond the surface, seeing each individual not just as a connection but as a brother or sister in Christ. This perspective shifts our approach from transactional interactions to genuine, heartfelt relationships, fostering an environment where mutual growth and support are rooted in love and respect. As we cultivate our networks with this mindset, we not only enrich our professional lives but also strengthen the fabric of our spiritual community, embodying the unity and love that Christ himself prayed for his followers in John 17:21, "that all of them may be one, Father, just as you are in me and I am in you."

By integrating these gospel-centered principles into our networking philosophy, we not only enhance our professional relationships but also contribute to a broader, more meaningful unity that reflects the love and peace of Christ in every interaction.

Make introductions. One of the most valuable things you can do for others is to make introductions. Help to connect people who you think could benefit from knowing each other and take the time to facilitate the introduction. This is a great way to provide value and be a matchmaker in your network. Making an introduction can be as simple and easy as sending an email introducing two people or companies you think could benefit each other.

When you're making introductions, leverage the principle of reciprocity—that innate sense we all have about not wanting to owe someone. While it shouldn't be your main motive for connecting others, it's a great side benefit: those you've helped often feel inclined to reciprocate. They might introduce you to their own contacts or be ready to lend you a hand in the future. The rationale behind networking is that everyone wins. It is not a zero-sum game, but a way for people to mutually help one another and gain greater successes for all parties involved. Consider the scriptural verse in Philippians 2:3-4, "Do nothing out of selfish ambition or vain conceit. Rather, in humility value others above yourselves, not looking to your own interests but each of you to the interests of the others." By helping those around you, you're investing in your future as much as theirs.

Outreach

Join professional organizations and attend events. Joining professional organizations and attending events is an excellent way to meet individuals in similar industries, expand your knowledge, and build relationships. Seek out events and organizations related to your field of interest and make an effort to participate and contribute. You can be both a mentee and a mentor.

Reach out to alums and mentors. Alumni and mentors can provide valuable insight, advice, and opportunities. Reach out to individuals who have been successful in your field and ask for their advice and support. They may also connect you with job opportunities and provide guidance on your career journey.

Participate in online communities. The internet has made it easier than ever to connect with others. Join online communities and forums related to your field and participate in discussions and activities. This is a great way to stay informed, build relationships, and expand your network.

Be proactive. Don't wait for opportunities to come to you, actively seek them out. Research companies and organizations that align with your interests and goals and reach out to them directly. Take the initiative to make things happen, and don't be afraid to put yourself out there.

Follow-up

Effective follow-up is a critical component of successful networking. Once you've made connections at events or meetings, keeping the momentum going by following up with those contacts is essential. A well-crafted email or LinkedIn message expressing gratitude for their time and reiterating your interest in staying connected can go a long way. This helps solidify your new relationships and keeps you top-of-mind for future opportunities or collaborations. Remember, follow-up is not a one-time event; it's an ongoing process of nurturing and cultivating meaningful connections.

Build Trust

To build a professional network, trust is crucial. You can establish trust and connection with others by focusing on shared interests and values rather than differences. Learning to relate to others in this way is essential to developing a strong network of colleagues and industry contacts.

To bridge the gap between the importance of follow-ups and the pivotal role of trust in building a professional network, consider this insightful quote from Stephen M. R. Covey's "The Speed of Trust": "Trust is the glue of life. It's the most essential ingredient in effective communication. It's the foundational principle that holds all relationships." This quote underscores that trust isn't just a nice-to-have; it's the cornerstone of all meaningful interactions and relationships. Establishing trust with someone isn't an overnight process—it's cultivated through consistent, authentic engagement over time.

Building trust, especially in a professional setting, demands focusing on what brings us together rather than what sets us apart. By emphasizing shared interests and values, we lay down the groundwork for genuine connections. It's through these connections that we're able to relate to our colleagues and industry contacts on a deeper level, essential for forging a resilient network. Engaging with individuals who share your passions and diving into meaningful conversations not only broadens your professional circle but also paves the way for future opportunities. Remember, the journey of building a network is a marathon, not a sprint, requiring time, dedication, and a sincere effort to connect with others in a way that's true to both you and them.

Networking Etiquette

Networking is all about building and maintaining professional relationships, and how you conduct yourself plays a crucial role in making a lasting impression. To succeed in networking, you need to be respectful, courteous, and mindful of social norms and cultural differences.

When attending networking events, it's important to make a good first impression. Arriving on time is a sign of respect for the host and shows that you're serious about making connections. Dressing appropriately and being well-groomed can help you feel confident and professional. Also, make sure you're prepared with business cards and your "be interesting" introduction that summarizes what you do.

When meeting new people, offer a firm handshake and maintain eye contact. These simple gestures can show that you're engaged and interested in building a relationship. Be attentive and actively listen to what others have to say. Show genuine interest in their business by asking thoughtful questions that show a sincere desire to learn about that person and what they do. Often, questions relating to what people find most fulfilling or intellectually stimulating will get them to open up and provide more information. These types of questions also help you to show that you care about that person and not just their work, which will help the relationship form more quickly.

The long-term effects of your networking efforts will yield much more fruit if you do more than simply collect business cards. Following up with the people you meet and keeping in touch can help create opportunities to collaborate, share ideas and knowledge, and build trust. Connect with them on social media or LinkedIn, and schedule follow-up meetings or calls to stay in touch.

Networking Success Story #1

A Simple Thank You Card

Abby had always been a firm believer in the power of networking and building genuine connections with people. She would always take the time to write a handwritten thank you card to anyone she met, no matter how small the encounter was. She felt that these small gestures were essential in building and maintaining relationships.

Abby never expected anything in return for her actions, but her persistence in sending these cards paid off in a big way. One day, she found herself at a large gathering at the governor's office. During the event, the topic of discussion turned to the lost art of writing thank you cards, and Abby was surprised to hear more than a dozen people in the room, all of whom were powerful individuals, speak about how they or someone they knew had received a card from her.

The group was impressed with Abby's dedication to building genuine connections, and they decided to invite her to speak to the governor's group on the topic. Abby accepted the invitation and shared her experiences and insights on networking and building relationships. Her presentation was well received, and one person in the group was so impressed that she offered Abby her dream job—working in the governor's mansion.

Abby was shocked and grateful for the opportunity that arose from her small act of kindness. She realized that her persistence in sending thank you cards had made a significant impact on her life and her career. From that day on, Abby continued to send cards, knowing that it could lead to something great. She learned that remembering important details, showing genuine interest in others, and following up are critical to life's successes, and she was a firm believer in the power of networking.

Following up with your networking connections can make a world of difference in building strong and lasting relationships. By using a combination of these methods, you can ensure that your follow-up efforts are effective and leave a positive and lasting impression.

Body language is an essential part of networking etiquette. Be aware of your nonverbal cues, as they can convey a lot about your attitude and level of engagement. Crossing your arms or slouching can be perceived as closed-off or disinterested, so instead, stand up straight and maintain an open posture to show that you're open to building a connection.

When it comes to networking, treating others with respect and courtesy is crucial. Be mindful of the topics you discuss and avoid sensitive or controversial subjects that could potentially cause offense or discomfort. It's generally best to avoid discussing politics, religion, or personal issues in a networking setting.

Being aware of cultural differences in communication styles is also essential. What may be considered polite or appropriate in one culture may be perceived as rude or disrespectful in another. Being aware of these cultural nuances can help you avoid miscommunications and show that you're respectful of others' beliefs and values.

In summary, being respectful and courteous to others is a critical component of successful networking. It involves avoiding sensitive or controversial topics, being aware of cultural differences in communication styles, and maintaining a polite and professional attitude. By following these guidelines, you can build lasting impressions and forge strong connections that will serve you well throughout your career. So, let's focus on building relationships and following these tips to set you on the right path to success!

CHAPTER 3

Developing a Strategic, Purpose-Driven Mindset

Being interesting can give you an edge in your personal and professional life. However, simply being interesting may not be enough. You need to be able to articulate your unique value proposition and differentiate yourself from others to stand out. This begins with determining your personal strategy and leveraging it in all your associations. Strategy is about winning and to win, you need to understand the rules of the game and where you fit in them. Start by asking yourself the four questions of strategy:

1. Where do I compete? From a personal standpoint this could be an industry that you want to work in, a product that you're trying to launch, or an impact that you want to make. Having a clear vision of your goals and where you need to be to realize them will allow you to have a more targeted approach to building your network. Though this may seem obvious, many people have goals that are far too broad, such as "make a lot of money", "become a CEO", or "start a company". Specific goals will lead to specific actions that will turn into specific results.

2. What is my unique value proposition? We've already touched on this, but it's crucial to understand that it's the core of any networking conversation. You've probably heard the saying that "everyone is in sales." Here's where that becomes practical. No matter your field or desired position,

being able to identify and communicate what makes you unique is essential for achieving your goals. Picture this in a networking context: imagine everyone you meet is an investor with limited resources. Your job is to persuade them that investing their time and energy in you is their best option. This is where your "Be Interesting Script" from chapter 2 comes in handy. By highlighting what makes you unique in an engaging way, you'll attract people's attention, significantly improving your chances of forming meaningful connections.

3. What resources and capabilities are necessary to create my unique value? Think about how you have gotten to where you are. What types of people, experiences, credentials, and other resources do you already have that you can leverage to get yourself to the next step in your life and career? What capabilities and skills have you garnered to create your unique value? An honest and comprehensive look into what you already have will provide some insight into the process of getting to the next step. Additionally, your resources and capabilities may be complementary to those of someone with whom you may wish to network. When parties bring something to the table, a stronger, symbiotic relationship can be formed. It amounts to the ethic version of "you scratch my back and I'll scratch yours".

4. How do I sustain my competitive advantage? If you're asking yourself this question in a networking scenario, you're already halfway there. Sustaining your competitive advantage means making sure that you continue to stand out amidst the crowd and be the person that gets the job, sells the product, or makes the impact. Building a strong network is one way to hedge against unknowns, giving you resources to get yourself back on top when setbacks occur. Industry or interest specific networks will also create synergies of information that will help you stay on top of trends and know what resources and capabilities to continually obtain to stay on top in the first place.

Although answering the four questions is critical to developing a personal strategy, it can be difficult to organize your thoughts and know how to communicate your unique value proposition clearly. One way to do this is by using the Competitive Advantage Pyramid (Dyer et al. 47), which can help you identify and communicate your strengths, values, and passions to others. By leveraging the insights gained from the Competitive Advantage Pyramid, you can create a compelling personal brand and position yourself for success. A competitive advantage pyramid can be an effective resource for developing a strategic, purpose-driven mindset and serving as a foundation for creating a "be interesting" script.

Example:

Walt Disney

Competitive Advantage Pyramid

ACTIVITIES
Create Animated, Family-Friendly Stories | Entertain! | Technological Innovation | Conservation | Create Family Experiences

RESOURCES, CAPABILITIES, & ORGANIZATION
Resources: Creativity | Vivid Imagination | Funding | Leverage | Location | Funny & Personable
Capabilities: Determination & Perseverance | Business Acumen | Animation | Marketing Genius

VALUES & PRIORITIES
Values: Family Centered | Hard Work | Optimism | Quality | Persistence
Priorities: Explore Imagination | Storytelling | Always Innovating | Entertainment | Honoring the Past

Mantra: If you can dream it, you can do it!

The base of the pyramid represents your values, mission, and priorities. These are the fundamental principles that guide your actions and decisions. They provide the foundation for your competitive advantage and should align with the company you wish to work for. When your values and mission are in harmony with the company, you can be confident that your actions will be aligned with their goals and objectives. Your values and mission should reflect what is important to you and what drives you. They should be the foundation for your professional and personal life. Values include concepts and ideas including integrity, lightheartedness, faith or spirituality, and commitment to environmental causes.

The pyramid's middle represents your resources and capabilities, also known as knowledge, skills, and abilities. These are the things that you bring to the table that differentiate you from others. They result from years of experience, education, and personal development. Your resources and capabilities can help you create a unique and compelling value proposition that sets you apart. Your skills, knowledge, and abilities should reflect your strengths and areas of expertise and should be leveraged to achieve your goals and purpose. Both soft and hard skills belong in this section. Capabilities might include being an empathetic leader, ability to speak two languages, and having an expertise in Microsoft Excel. Resources are items beyond you that you can draw upon to accomplish your goals. Those include things like a strong social network, access to capital and financial means, or a robust alum network.

The top of the pyramid represents your activities, the things you do to achieve your goals and realize your purpose. Your values, mission, and resources and capabilities direct your activities and help you focus on what is most important. When your activities are aligned with your competitive advantage pyramid, they become a driver for creating and sustaining success. Your activities should reflect your priorities, and should be chosen to align with your values, mission, and resources and capabilities.

This should be a familiar concept as you research successful companies and organizations you wish to be a part of. Every company is built on a set of values and priorities that drives it to accomplish a goal. Think of Walmart's slogan "Save Money, Live Better". Walmart advertises values of frugality, utility, and meeting the needs of the average person. To make those values actionable, it relies on its resource pool of stores, fleets, supplier relationships, and consumer goodwill. Due to its size, Walmart is capable of offering some of the lowest prices on the market and has perfected its marketing approach for its target market. These resources and capabilities are all built around living up to its values and accomplishing its core activity of making money by providing goods to the mid-to-low end of the market. As you look at your own competitive advantage pyramid, make sure that you are likewise accomplishing your desired activities by developing resources and capabilities that align with your values.

If we consider the Walt Disney example from earlier, ask yourself "does the current Walt Disney Corporation 2024 mission align with the mission, values, capabilities, resources and activities below of Walt?"

The mission of The Walt Disney Company is to entertain, inform and inspire people around the globe through the power of unparalleled storytelling, reflecting the iconic brands, creative minds and innovative technologies that make ours the world's premier entertainment company (The Walt Disney Company, 2024).

Creating a competitive advantage pyramid is a valuable exercise for anyone looking to develop a strategic, purpose-driven mindset. By aligning your values, mission, resources, and capabilities with the company you wish to work for, you can create a unique and compelling value proposition that sets you apart from others.

This, in turn, will help you create a "be interesting" script that showcases your skills and abilities and makes you stand out from the competition. By taking the time to develop your competitive advantage pyramid, you can create a roadmap for success and a foundation for your personal and professional life.

Incorporating Stewardship into Your Strategic Mindset

As we delve into the intricacies of developing a strategic mindset, it's crucial to recognize the role of stewardship in shaping our approach to business and personal growth. Stewardship, a principle deeply rooted in gospel teachings, emphasizes the importance of managing the resources, talents, and opportunities entrusted to us with care, integrity, and a sense of responsibility. This concept aligns perfectly with the foundational layer of our competitive advantage pyramid, where values, mission, and purpose serve as guiding principles.

Understanding ourselves as stewards in both our professional and personal lives encourages us to look beyond mere success metrics. It invites us to consider how we can use our unique value propositions, resources, and capabilities to serve others and contribute to the greater good. The Parable of the

Talents (Matthew 25:14-30) is not just a lesson in utilizing our gifts but a call to action to multiply the impact of these gifts through diligent stewardship.

By integrating the principle of stewardship into our strategic mindset, we begin to see our careers, our networks, and our personal ambitions not just as avenues for personal achievement but as platforms for meaningful contribution. This perspective not only enriches our understanding of success but also deepens the relationships we build along the way. As we align our activities with our values, mission, and the broader principle of stewardship, we create a more fulfilling and purpose-driven path to achieving our goals.

In essence, stewardship transforms the competitive advantage pyramid from a tool for personal advancement into a blueprint for living a life of purpose, service, and impact. As we navigate the complexities of business and personal development, let us embrace stewardship as a core component of our strategic, purpose-driven mindset, ensuring that our journey is not only about where we compete or how we stand out but about how we contribute to the world around us.

CHAPTER 4

Networking for Introverts

If you're an introvert, the idea of networking can be daunting. Small talk, large crowds, and the pressure to make connections can be overwhelming, and the thought of attending networking events can cause anxiety. However, it's possible for introverts to succeed in networking by playing to their strengths. Ether 12:27, from the Book of Mormon, reminds us "And if men come unto me I will show unto them their weakness. I give unto men weakness that they may be humble; and my grace is sufficient for all men that humble themselves before me; for if they humble themselves before me, and have faith in me, then will I make weak things become strong unto them." In this chapter, we'll explore some strategies for introverts to network effectively, turn weaknesses to strengths, and build strong professional relationships.

Start Small

If you're new to networking or just feel overwhelmed by the idea of attending large events, start small. Reach out to people in your immediate circle, such as coworkers or friends, and ask for introductions to people in their network. You can also attend smaller, more intimate events or gatherings where you are more likely to feel comfortable and be able to make meaningful connections. Attending a community event is a great way to start. Events such as church services, community parties, or service activities are often open to everyone and allow people to connect in a casual environment. There are likely people in the community who could be valuable resources for you personally or professionally, and making informal connections can lead to introductions or being invited to join a larger social circle.

One-on-one meetings are another way to get to know people in quieter, more controlled environments. As you reach out on LinkedIn, or as people offer to connect you to their contacts, request a brief 15-30 min. meeting where you can get to know the person and either discuss a relevant topic or get advice. Networking interactions with specific purposes help to break the ice and make the conversation occur more naturally. Additionally, people love to share what they know and be seen as an expert in something, so this type of meeting will ideally cause the person whom you meet with to take up most of the talking time, reducing the pressure on you. Even if you don't get all you need from that meeting, it will help potentially start an ongoing relationship that will yield fruit in the future.

Plan Ahead

For introverts, preparation can be key to making networking events less daunting. Before attending an event, do some research on who will be there and what the focus of the event is. This will give you a better sense of what to expect and help you prepare some talking points or questions ahead of time. You can also plan to arrive early, which will give you a chance to acclimate to the environment before it becomes too crowded.

Focus on Quality, not Quantity

Introverts tend to be more selective about their relationships and prefer to have a few close connections rather than a large network of acquaintances.

When networking, focus on building quality relationships rather than trying to meet as many people as possible. This can mean spending more time getting to know a few people at an event, rather than trying to collect as many business cards as possible.

Play to Your Strengths

One of the advantages of being an introvert is that you tend to be a good listener and observer. Use this to your advantage in networking situations by asking thoughtful questions, actively listening to others, and observing body language and other cues.

Follow Up on Your Connections

For introverts, building and maintaining relationships can be a slow and steady process. However, following up on your connections can be an effective way to build trust and deepen your relationships over time. Send a personalized email or handwritten note to someone you've met at a networking event or schedule a follow-up coffee or lunch to continue the conversation.

Use Social Media to Your Advantage

Social media can be a useful tool for introverts to network and build relationships without the pressure of face-to-face interactions. Consider joining online groups or communities related to your industry, where you can share ideas, ask questions, and connect with like-minded professionals. You can also use LinkedIn to research potential contacts and reach out to them in a low-pressure way.

Networking can be a challenging but rewarding experience for introverts. By playing to your strengths, focusing on quality relationships, and using preparation and follow-up to your advantage, you can build a strong professional network that supports your career goals.

Networking Success Story #2

In the world of networking for introverts, Ben's journey stands out as a powerful example of the benefits of stepping outside one's comfort zone, even when it doesn't feel natural. Ben, much like many introverts, found networking to be a daunting endeavor. For Ben, the prospect of small talk, large crowds, and the quest for meaningful connections was about as enticing as undergoing a root canal. Yet, his efforts underscores a pivotal strategy discussed in this chapter: starting small and embracing opportunities for meaningful engagement.

Ben stumbled upon a job posting for a research apprenticeship at his college, a position that instantly made him think of his friend Samuel, seemingly the ideal candidate. Acting on the impulse to help, Ben informed Samuel about the opportunity, embodying the principle of leveraging one's immediate circle to foster connections. Later, driven by a blend of curiosity and perhaps a dash of serendipity, Ben decided to apply for the position himself.

The interview day arrived, and Ben, armed with little more than his innate curiosity and the hope of making a meaningful impression, walked into the interview room. To his surprise, the interviewer was not a stranger but a familiar face from a campus club event he had attended—despite his reservations and introverted nature. This encounter was not merely a coincidence but a manifestation of the advice to attend smaller, more intimate events where meaningful connections are more likely to be made. Ben's decision to attend that club event weeks prior, despite his initial reluctance, was a step toward expanding his social circle in a manageable, less intimidating way.

During the interview, the recognition and subsequent pleasant conversation between Ben and the interviewer highlighted another strength of introverts: the ability to listen and engage in thoughtful dialogue. Ben's genuine interaction with the club president at the event, and now during the interview, showcased his ability to make a lasting impression through authentic engagement rather than superficial exchanges.

In the end, Ben landed the job, a win he credits to that one decision to attend the club's networking event. This outcome not only illustrates the importance of stepping out of one's comfort zone but also reinforces the chapter's guidance on focusing on quality, not quantity, in networking efforts. Ben's story is a reminder that for introverts, meaningful connections often stem from quality interactions and the courage to embrace opportunities for engagement, no matter how small or inconsequential they may seem at the time.

Sadly, Samuel didn't get the job, even though he seemed perfect for it on paper. This twist in the story highlights a key point: networking is unpredictable, and it's often those personal connections that make the difference, not just skills or experience. It's a statistic that bears repeating: 85% of jobs are secured through personal connections.

CHAPTER 5

Networking through Life Phases

Networking is a fun and exciting way to make new connections that can help you personally and professionally. It's all about building relationships with people who can help you achieve your goals, whether making new friends, finding a new job, or growing your business.

Networking for Teens

Teaching youth about consociating from a young age is important. You can start by explaining how important it is to build relationships and how much fun it can be to meet interesting people with great backgrounds and stories. It's important to remind them that networking is not about using people or trying to get something for nothing but building mutually beneficial relationships.

One of the most important things about networking is communicating well. Your child should learn to talk to people and listen to them too. They should also learn how to express their interests and goals in a way that is respectful of others.

Another great thing about networking is building connections. Teaching your teen how to make new friends and strengthen existing relationships is essential. They can do this by being proactive and reaching out to new acquaintances through social media, joining clubs or groups, or volunteering. Doing so will help them build a vast network of connections they can call on for support and advice in the future.

Teach your teen to serve and be helpful. They should learn that building relationships is not just about what they can get out of it but also about what they can give. They should know how to help others by offering their skills, knowledge, or resources and how to be a good friend, colleague, or mentor. Mosiah 2:17 summarizes this sentiment perfectly, "And behold, I tell you these things that ye may learn wisdom; that ye may learn that when ye are in the service of your fellow beings ye are only in the service of your God."

Teach your teen about networking etiquette. They should know how to introduce themselves, safely exchange contact information, and follow up appropriately. They should also learn how to respect other people's time and space and accept rejection gracefully.

Lastly, and most importantly, young people must be aware of their safety when engaging in online activities, particularly when building their networks and relationships. While the internet provides many opportunities for socializing, learning, and creating, it also poses various risks, such as cyberbullying, exposure to inappropriate content, and online predators. As such, parents, educators, coaches, and mentors should take an active role in helping teens navigate the online world safely.

One of the most important aspects of online safety is education. Teens should be taught early on the potential risks of online activities and how to avoid or respond to them. This can include preparing them about online privacy, safe passwords, and how to identify and report inappropriate behavior. Parents and educators can also use filtering and monitoring software to help keep teens safe.

Parents and educators should encourage teens to engage in positive and productive online activities, such as learning, creating, and connecting with others who share their interests. This can promote a healthy and balanced use of technology while reducing the risk of negative online experiences.

It is essential for teens to be aware of the potential risks and benefits of online activities and to be equipped with the skills and knowledge needed to navigate the online world safely. By working together, parents and educators can help teens build positive relationships and networks online while also ensuring their safety and well-being.

Engaging in networking presents an enjoyable and thrilling opportunity to encounter unfamiliar faces and establish valuable associations, beneficial both in personal and professional circles. As a parent, it becomes crucial to instill in teenagers an understanding of networking from an early stage, explaining the significance of cultivating relationships, proficient communication, forging connections, serving others, and adhering to networking etiquette. By doing so, your adolescent will enjoy the process of constructing a robust network of friends, fostering mutual support, and propelling themselves towards their goals.

Networking in High School

Networking is an essential skill that can benefit high school students in many ways, such as finding internships, getting into college, and even landing a job after graduation. The earlier you start networking, the more opportunities you will have. Here are some tips on how high school students can begin networking:

- By joining clubs and extracurricular activities, you have the chance to connect with individuals who share your interests and passions. This shared bond creates a sense of belonging and allows for meaningful relationships to form. As you participate in these activities, you'll learn valuable skills and gain experiences that can benefit you both personally and professionally. Moreover, these connections can be instrumental in helping you achieve your goals and aspirations.

- Attend networking events: Attend networking events relevant to your interests or career aspirations. This can include college fairs, career fairs, and industry-specific events. These events allow you to meet professionals in your desired field and learn about potential career paths.

31

- Volunteer: Volunteering is an excellent way to gain valuable skills and experience while giving back to the community. It is also a great way to meet people from different backgrounds and industries who can help you achieve your goals.

- Utilize social media: Social media is an effective platform for networking. Create a professional online presence by creating a LinkedIn profile and connecting with professionals in your desired field. You can also join groups related to your interests and participate in discussions.

- Reach out to people you admire: Don't be afraid to reach out to people you admire and respect. This can be accomplished by sending an email, a message on LinkedIn, or even a direct message on social media. Explain your interest in their work and ask for advice. Remember always—safety first! Keep parents informed of who you connect with through technology and social media platforms. Never meet anyone you don't know in anything other than a public, safe location.

- Practice good communication: Communication is vital when it comes to networking. Learn how to effectively convey your interests and goals while being respectful of others. Always follow up after meeting someone new and keep in touch.

- Consider doing internships: High school students can also gain valuable experience and build connections by participating in internships. Look for opportunities in industries or fields that interest you and reach out to local businesses or organizations to see if they have any available internships. This can provide you with valuable skills and experience, and can also help you build relationships with professionals in your desired field.

Networking is an essential skill that high school students can begin to develop early on. By joining clubs and extracurricular activities, attending networking events, volunteering, utilizing social media, reaching out to people you admire, and practicing good communication, students can start building a strong network of connections that can help them achieve their goals in the future.

Networking in College

Once upon a time, on a college campus full of young minds eager to learn, a new app called Nouri.ai made its grand debut. And what did it offer? A free slice of pizza for every student who downloaded it! What a deal, right?

But here's the thing, the freshmen and sophomores were still trying to figure out their way around campus and didn't give the offer a second thought. They were too busy exploring and making new friends to worry about networking. Little did they know, they were missing out on a valuable opportunity.

On the other hand, the juniors and seniors were seasoned pros, and they knew a good thing when they saw it. They quickly downloaded the app and grabbed a slice of that delicious pizza. And as they started using it, they soon realized that Nouri.ai was a game-changer in networking. They could connect with alums, industry professionals, and peers in their field with just a few clicks. It was like having a personal networking fairy on their phone!

The juniors and seniors felt the urgency of building a network and didn't waste any time. They happily shared their experiences with the freshmen and sophomores, explaining the importance of networking and how Nouri.ai made it so easy. And just like that, the lightbulb went off for the younger students, and they too joined the networking party.

So, there you have it, folks; a story of how a free slice of pizza turned into valuable connections and a lesson in the importance of networking. The takeaway? Networking is a serious business, but it doesn't have to be all work and no play. With the right tools, building a network can be a piece of cake—or in this case, pizza!

Your peers play a crucial role in your college and career success. It's almost impossible to claim that you have achieved everything alone. Along the way, classmates, professors, and fellow students will continue contributing to your academic and professional successes. We need others to succeed.

Networking is more than just a buzzword; it's a vital part of college. The connections you make today will be the ones that will help you land your dream job or secure a scholarship. Joining clubs, attending events, and participating in class discussions will help you build your network.

Nowadays, social media makes it easier than ever to connect with others. From LinkedIn to Facebook, plenty of platforms allow you to connect and communicate with people in your field of interest. Joining groups and communities related to your field can help you expand your network and get to know people with similar goals.

Networking is a process that requires effort and dedication, but it can also be enjoyable and rewarding. It's not just about finding a job; it's about making meaningful connections, gaining new insights, and expanding your horizons. By putting in the effort to build strong relationships with others, you can open doors to new opportunities and experiences. So, approach networking with a positive attitude and a willingness to learn and grow, and you'll be amazed at the benefits it can bring.

Whenever you're tempted to avoid networking—because honestly, it's not easy—remind yourself of the many benefits you can gain from making valuable and meaningful networking connections. Here are ten helpful tips for networking in college:

1. Attend networking events: Networking events hosted on college campuses are an excellent way for students to connect with professionals from various industries, majors, and fields. During these events, be prepared to share your contact details by texting, emailing, sharing or linking them, or even handing out copies of your resume. Since most students do not have a business card at this stage in life, electronic business cards or simply sharing your mobile phone's contact card will suffice. Even if you don't immediately secure a job or internship, these contacts can be instrumental in helping you in the future.

2. Get involved in clubs and organizations: Joining clubs and organizations is an excellent way to meet like-minded individuals and build relationships. It also shows potential employers that you are a well-rounded individual with various interests.

3. Utilize LinkedIn: LinkedIn is a premier platform for social media-based networking. Create a professional profile, connect with professionals

in your desired field, and join groups related to your interests. This is a great way to stay informed about industry trends and learn about job opportunities.

4. Reach out to alums: Many colleges have an alumni network that can be accessed through their career center. Reach out to alums working in your desired field and ask for their advice. They can provide valuable insights and connect you with job opportunities.

5. Volunteer: Volunteering is a great way to gain experience, build relationships, and give back to the community. It also shows employers that you are a committed and hardworking individual. Look for volunteer opportunities that align with your interests and career goals.

6. Build a personal brand: Develop a personal brand that showcases your skills, experiences, and passions. Use your personal website, social media, and other platforms to showcase your work and tell your story. This will make you stand out to potential employers and help you build a professional reputation.

7. Take the initiative: Don't wait for opportunities to come to you. Actively seek them out. Research companies and organizations that align with your interests and goals, and contact them directly.

8. Network in your classes: You never know where your next opportunity may come. Take advantage of the diverse student body in your classes and build relationships with your classmates. You can collaborate on projects, or they might know someone who can help you achieve your goals.

9. Follow up: After networking events and meetings, following up with the contacts you have made is important. Send an email or LinkedIn message to thank them for their time and let them know you are interested in staying in touch.

10. Leverage your network: Once you have built a network of contacts, don't be afraid to ask for help. Reach out to your contacts when you are looking for job opportunities, advice, or industry insights. Remember that networking is a two-way street; always be willing to help others as

well. "As iron sharpens iron, so one person sharpens another," Proverbs 27:17.

Networking Success Story #3

You Never Know Who You'll be Talking To

Emily was always looking for opportunities to network. She understood the power of building relationships and the impact it could have on her future. During her time in college, she made an effort to meet as many people in her classes as possible and joined several clubs and social events. She knew that one day, she might be able to help someone with a job or introduction, and perhaps they could help her in return.

At a club meeting, Emily was speaking with a professor from another major. She saw this as an opportunity to share her 60-second "be interesting" script, which included her goal of working for Adobe. Little did she know, the professor had a long-standing relationship with Adobe and was able to connect her directly to the Vice President in charge of creative content. The professor recommended her for the job, and Emily was hired on the spot.

Emily was grateful for her networking efforts and the impact they had on her future. She learned that by putting herself out there and making an effort to meet people, she could create opportunities that she never thought possible. From that day on, Emily continued to attend networking events and build relationships with those around her, knowing that one day, those connections could lead to something great.

CHAPTER 6

Tools of the Trade

As you may have realized, successful networking requires focused effort and a myriad of skills that can seem a bit daunting at times. Furthermore, once you gain the skillset and put in the effort, sometimes it can become difficult to know where to focus your search for the correct people and target your search. The good news is that you are not alone. Starting with the most basic tools and evolving with technology, there are many resources that make finding, meeting, and connecting with people easier than ever. Some of the smartest, most capable people in the world go unnoticed due to lack of the right network. These tools can help you avoid that trap and take advantage of the synergies and opportunities that networks provide.

Business Cards

In Japan, it is considered polite to use both hands when accepting a business card as there is a high emphasis on status in Japanese culture. Having a prominent job title on your business card can give you an advantage in business. While there are no specific etiquette guidelines for receiving and giving business cards in Western cultures, it is important to be aware that certain practices may be considered offensive in other cultures.

Business cards remain relevant in a virtual world, as they provide a personal touch and create a sense of trust between individuals. They can also be used as powerful networking tools. Through design elements, a business card can convey information about the individual or business, and according to a study from the Statistic Brain Research Institute, 72% of people form an opinion about a company based on the quality of their business card (Statistic Brain Research Institute).

Statistics show that first impressions are determined by 55% the way you dress, act, and walk through the door, 38% the quality of your voice, grammar, and confidence, and 7% the words you choose to say (Heunis, 2022). You only have a few seconds to make or break that first impression (Ambady, 1992).

Investing in a professional and well-designed business card can help market your personality, skills, and company. Always keep business cards with you, as you never know when a potential connection may arise in unexpected places such as airport lounges or standing in lines. Use them as an opportunity to strike up a conversation and leave a lasting impression.

To take your networking to the next level, you may consider investing in a Popl, Dot, or using the Nouri.ai QRConnect code to create an electronic business card. These e-cards are usually linked to a webpage that allows the recipient of your phone's bump or scan to access the page and easily download your contact details to their contacts app. By having an electronic business card, you can make it more convenient for people to add you to their network, while also showing that you are tech-savvy and up to date with modern networking trends.

On two separate occasions, I've had the opportunity to meet Lew Cramer, the CEO of Colliers International. Lew is a wonderful man with a smile that immediately puts those around him at ease. In the two times we've met, separated by several months, he immediately presented me with his business card. He genuinely wants to connect with everyone he meets. In those two events, one was a networking event and the other was when a colleague and I bumped into him in a restaurant. He was meeting a high-ranking politician and made it a point to stop by our booth on his way out. Leave an impression as Lew did—genuine connection, willingness to share his contact details, and be friendly and smile!

Social Media

Gone are the days when social media earned a reputation for being a waste of time and effort. Now, with a pool of millions who share your interest and field, finding the right people to network with is just one click of a mouse. Social media is not just a game changer for the way you get connected to people—it also changes the way you nurture the network you build.

Making an Impact in Social Media

We spend too much time watching our network without truly engaging with them. Social media is a great platform to see what people in our network are doing. Many people post updates about their personal lives, such as special occasions, life events, and accomplishments.

Social media is an outlet for people to express themselves or present themselves differently than they are in real life. Engaging in social media can be therapeutic and even an escape from our daily routine. In the past decade, people have been monetizing their social media through affiliate programs, sponsorships, and interactions with their audience. This shows how much people want to connect with others.

Let's take Facebook birthdays as an example. To be honest, I am not always the best with dates. There have been times when I have forgotten important dates simply because I was caught up with the mountains of tasks in front of me. Facebook has since saved me from experiencing the embarrassment of missing celebrations.

Here's the thing, Facebook birthday reminders seem to have taken away our ability to let our sincerity transcend through our words. Now, we write a pithy, repetitive phrase on the day of someone's birthday on their Facebook wall and move on with our day. Most likely, we didn't even know it was the person's birthday. We were mindlessly scanning Facebook and were reminded of a loved one's or friend's birthday the day of their birthday. Perhaps we add a little love emoji or celebration balloon to distinguish ourselves from the other "Happy Birthday" posts. The effort is unremarkable and quickly forgetful.

LinkedIn has even gotten into the game now by reminding us of birthdays—again, on the day of the person's birthday. Social media companies don't fully appreciate the importance of recognizing someone on their "special day." Can we blame them though? After all—they created the monster that is social media. What is intriguing about LinkedIn storing birthday data and using it to remind us of a connection's birthday is that they too recognize the importance of celebrating a birthday as a matter of building a business relationship. They too fall short of actually making it useful to the LinkedIn user, but at least they acknowledge the business significance of that data point.

A lot of gurus and experts dispense the best ways to impress our network, but the truth is connecting and leaving a mark on social media can be linked to one thing—going the extra mile. This includes writing a personal note, being genuine with our message, and replacing spam messages with words that can make them feel acknowledged and valued.

Using Social Media to Grow Your Network

Professional networking has been revolutionized by the rise of social media. Whether you're a small business owner, an entrepreneur, or just looking to expand your professional circle, social media can help you connect with others in your industry and open new doors for your career. In this section, we'll explore how you can use social media to grow your network and take your career to the next level. From building a professional profile to collaborating with others, we'll provide you with practical tips and strategies for making the most of social media for networking.

Build a professional profile: Make sure your social media profiles are professional and showcase your skills and interests. Use a clear headshot and write a compelling bio that highlights your expertise.

- Connect with others: Use social media to connect with people in your industry, join groups and communities related to your field, and engage in conversations.

- Share valuable content: Share valuable and relevant content with your network. This will help establish you as a thought leader in your industry and attract new connections.

- Attend virtual events: Many events and conferences are now held online, attend them, and use them as an opportunity to connect with other attendees.

- Network on LinkedIn: LinkedIn is the professional social media platform, use it to connect with other professionals in your industry and expand your network.

- Collaborate with others: Collaborating with other professionals in your industry can be a great way to grow your network and gain visibility.

- Follow and engage with influencers: Following and engaging with influencers in your industry can help you connect with their followers and expand your network.

- Be consistent: Consistently posting, engaging, and networking on social media will help you build a strong network over time.

Facebook

- Monthly active users: 2.958 billion (We Are Social, 2023)
- Largest age group: 25-34 (26.3%)
- Gender: 44% female, 56% male
- Time spent per day: 38 minutes

Facebook caters to a diverse user base, including millennials, baby boomers, and Gen X. The platform offers various networking tools like event creation, widgets, fundraisers, and app integrations. Its groups feature serves as a networking goldmine, with over 2.9 billion users participating in groups matching their interests and goals.

Instagram

- Monthly active users: 2 billion (We Are Social, 2023)
- Largest age group: 25-34 (33.1%)
- Gender: 57% female, 43% male
- Average time spent per day: 29 minutes

Instagram, a visual platform popular among all ages, supports professional networking by allowing users to showcase products, services, and skills. Features like hashtags, stories, and the Instagram Live Video feature help expand reach, while the platform's search function facilitates finding industry connections. Instagram Pods, or groups, provide opportunities for collaboration and support.

X

- Daily active users: 556 million (We Are Social, 2023)
- Largest age group: 30-49 (44%)
- Gender: 32% female, 68% male

X, a microblogging platform, is ideal for staying informed and connecting with others in your industry. Users can join conversations through hashtags and create curated lists of accounts. Features like Reposting and live-streaming events promote interaction and connection.

LinkedIn

- Monthly active users: 310 million (We Are Social, 2023)
- Largest age group: 46-55
- Gender: 51% male, 49% female
- Time spent per day: 11 minutes

LinkedIn, a professional networking platform, offers tools like endorsements, recommendations, and job applications. Users can engage with companies and alumni, while LinkedIn Groups facilitate collaboration, information sharing, and support.

TikTok

- Monthly active users: 1.051 billion (We Are Social, 2023)
- Largest age group: 18-24
- Gender: 59% female, 41% male
- Time spent per day: 45+ minutes

TikTok, primarily used for short-form videos, is helpful for creative industries. The platform encourages content creation, collaboration through the Duet feature, and engagement via live streaming.

YouTube

- Monthly active users: 2.514 billion (We Are Social, 2023)
- Largest age group: 15-25
- Gender: 72% of all female internet users and 72% of all male internet users
- Time spent per day: 41.9 minutes among viewers 18 and older

YouTube supports networking through video creation, playlists, live streaming, and community building. Users can monetize content and engage with others through various features.

Snapchat

- Monthly active users: 635 million (We Are Social, 2023)
- Largest age group: 13-34 (75%)
- Gender: 58% female, 40% male
- Time spent per day: 26 minutes

Snapchat, popular among creative industries, offers features like Stories, Snap Map, and live streaming for content sharing and real-time audience engagement.

Pinterest

- Monthly active users: 445 million (We Are Social, 2023)
- Largest age group: 30-49
- Gender: 78% female, 22% male
- Time spent per day: 14.2 minutes

Pinterest, a platform for sharing ideas, is ideal for creative industries. Users can create boards, save and share content, and engage with others through groups and communities. The platform's search function allows users to discover new ideas and connect with others based on their interests.

Reddit

- Monthly active users: 430 million (We Are Social, 2023)
- Largest age group: 18-29 (38%)
- Gender: 69% male, 31% female
- Time spent per day: 16.4 minutes

Reddit, known as "the front page of the internet," provides opportunities for users to engage in topic-specific communities called subreddits. These subreddits facilitate networking, collaboration, and knowledge sharing within various industries and interests.

Clubhouse

- Monthly active users: 10 million (We Are Social, 2023)
- Largest age group: 25-34
- Gender: 48% female, 52% male
- Time spent per day: 11 minutes

Clubhouse, an audio-based social media app, allows users to join and create virtual rooms for discussions, interviews, and presentations. The platform encourages networking through conversations, collaborations, and connecting with others in specific industries or with shared interests.

Quora

- Monthly active users: 300 million (We Are Social, 2023)
- Largest age group: 18-34
- Gender: 66% male, 34% female
- Time spent per day: 5.5 minutes

Quora, a question-and-answer platform, enables users to showcase their expertise and knowledge within their industries. By answering questions and engaging in discussions, users can establish themselves as thought leaders and network with professionals in their field.

It's human nature to crave connection with others. Therefore, it's not surprising that a significant amount of research and development has gone into creating ways to connect people. Social media has become a popular way for people to fulfill their need for meaningful and genuine human connections. By using social media strategically, we can build and strengthen relationships with others. A small gesture such as a "like" or comment can go a long way in showing someone you're thinking of them and remember them.

Artificial Intelligence

Artificial intelligence (AI) is the latest tool that can be harnessed to find the right people to reach out to in our search for great connections. AI is revolutionizing networking by leveraging its capabilities in learning, problem-solving, and decision-making. AI's statistical models and data analysis enable it to identify patterns, predict outcomes, and automate tasks, making it a potent force in expanding networks, managing connections, and personalizing interactions.

Within this realm, we'll delve into AI-powered networking tools, which facilitate quick network expansion and connections aligned with your career objectives. Furthermore, we'll discuss how AI can effectively manage your existing network and offer insights on strengthening crucial relationships. Lastly, we'll explore how AI can enhance the personalization of your networking efforts, cultivating stronger and more meaningful professional connections.

AI-Powered Networking Tools

AI-powered networking tools are designed to help you identify and connect with new people in your industry or field. These tools use AI algorithms to analyze your existing network and suggest new contacts relevant to your interests or goals. By using these tools, you can quickly and easily expand your network and connect with people who can help you achieve your career objectives.

There are a variety of AI-powered networking tools available, including:

Networking Apps

These apps use AI to suggest new contacts based on your professional interests and goals, allowing you to discover valuable connections within your industry.

AI-Powered Chatbots

These chatbots can handle routine networking tasks, such as sending follow-up messages or scheduling meetings, helping you manage connections effortlessly.

Social Media Platforms

Leveraging AI algorithms, social media platforms suggest new connections and facilitate relationship-building with key influencers in your industry.

Leveraging AI to Manage Your Network

AI can also be used to manage your existing network of contacts. For example, some networking platforms use AI-powered algorithms to identify key relationships within your network and suggest ways to strengthen those connections. These algorithms can also help you identify potential networking opportunities and guide you in nurturing relationships that are most important to your career.

In addition, AI-powered tools can help you stay up to date with your network by tracking changes in your contacts, job titles, companies, and professional interests. By staying on top of these changes, you can better understand your contacts' needs and identify new ways to add value to your professional relationships.

Personalizing Your Networking with AI

One of the most powerful features of AI in networking is its ability to personalize interactions with your network. For example, some networking platforms use AI to analyze your contacts' professional interests and suggest ways to start a conversation or collaborate on a project. This personalization helps you build stronger and more meaningful relationships with your contacts, which can lead to new opportunities and career growth.

Here are just a few:

LinkedIn—LinkedIn uses AI to suggest articles, posts, and people that may be of interest to you based on your activity and connections. It also uses AI to match job postings with relevant candidates based on their profiles, skills, and endorsements.

Humin—Humin is a mobile app that uses AI to help you manage your contacts and build relationships. It automatically organizes your contacts by how often you communicate with them and suggests times and ways to follow up.

Introhive—Introhive is a relationship intelligence platform that uses AI to analyze your contacts and suggest ways to strengthen your relationships. It can identify key relationships within your network and suggest ways to nurture those connections.

Crystal—Crystal is a browser extension that uses AI to analyze public data and suggest ways to communicate with people based on their communication style. It can help you personalize your messages and improve your chances of getting a response.

Nouri.ai—Nouri.ai is an AI-powered networking platform that helps you build relationships with professionals in your industry. It uses AI to identify key connections and suggest ways to strengthen those relationships. It can also help you personalize your interactions with your network and identify new opportunities for growth. As the author of this book and the CEO of Nouri, I can attest to its strengths in helping one build relationships for success in life and in business.

AI can also help you tailor your networking efforts to specific industries or regions. For example, some networking platforms use AI to identify trends and emerging opportunities in your industry and suggest ways to build relationships with key players in those areas. By leveraging these insights, you can make more informed decisions about where to focus your networking efforts and build relationships that are most relevant to your career.

AI-powered networking tools have the potential to enhance your professional network and accelerate your journey to achieving your career goals. By using AI to find new contacts, manage your existing network, and personalize your interactions, you can build stronger and more meaningful relationships with your professional contacts.

CHAPTER 7

Maintaining Your Network

When you open your contacts app on your Google or iPhone, take a moment to scroll through the list of names. Do you struggle to recognize anyone, or are there names of people you haven't spoken to in months or even years? Are the photos of them up-to-date, and are you sure their contact details are still accurate? If you sent out holiday cards this year, did any come back undeliverable because they've moved? Additionally, do your contacts contain numerous duplicates of the same person? Our relationships are like plants; they need nurturing, cultivating, and deserve our time and attention. Similar to the advice in Jacob 5:66, we must clear away branches that no longer bear fruit, dutifully pruning our network to foster healthier, more productive connections.

Keeping Your Contacts Current and Relevant

The Purge

In my research of over 4,000,000 people stored in contact apps like Google Contacts or iPhone Contacts, I've found that most people have very little information about the people in these apps. In fact, the vast majority of people only have a name and phone number, about one in four have an email associated, and even fewer have photos. Rarely do people use the other fields in the contact app to capture important information about the person or business, even though fields like "Birthdate, notes, and social media" are available. The people we store in our contacts app are just that—contacts. If it were for storing relationships, we might capture better information to help us build those relationships. We could use the contacts app to manage our relationships, but truthfully, the apps are not created to handle those relationship-building tasks. If we need to make a call or "get in touch" with someone, the contacts app does just what it is intended to do: contact.

Just like my friend who was trying to convince his wife that he needed a bigger garage because the old one "does not work as well as before," networking can feel like that too. Making connections and building relationships can feel like storing what we think are "much-needed" items in our "networking" garage. It seems harmless, never going to be a problem, until it becomes one. One day, we wake up with connections that are unrelated to the things we want to pursue or names we can't even remember. Just like my friend's garage, it's essential to take the time to clean out our "contact garages" and focus on building relationships with people that truly matter.

Cleaning House

Maintaining a strong and relevant network is essential to personal and professional success. One way to ensure that your connections align with your goals is to regularly engage in a process known as a "purge". A purge involves reviewing your contacts list and carefully evaluating who will positively impact your business, personal life, and overall objectives.

Marie Kondo's book "The Life-Changing Magic of Tidying Up" (Kondo, 2014) centers around the idea of only keeping items that "spark joy" in your life. In the book, Kondo emphasizes the importance of organizing your possessions in a specific order, beginning with clothing, and moving on to books, papers, miscellaneous items, and sentimental items.

One of the unique aspects of Kondo's approach is her emphasis on the emotional impact of possessions. By focusing on the joy that items bring our lives, rather than their practical or functional value, Kondo encourages readers to let go of items that may be holding them back, causing them stress, or keeping them from important things in life. The book also touches on the idea that organizing and decluttering can positively impact mental and emotional well-being and help create a sense of peace and calm in the home. Likewise, we need to take a similar emotional approach to our connections. If, upon reviewing a connection for the 'keep' or 'toss' pile, we ask ourselves, 'Does this connection "spark joy"?' If the answer is no, perhaps it's time to let it go. Having 4,000 contacts is impressive but not conducive to building positive and rewarding relationships.

The Dunbar theory (ScienceDirect, 2022), named after British anthropologist Robin Dunbar, proposes that the human brain can maintain around 150 meaningful relationships. While widely accepted as a benchmark for building and maintaining personal and professional relationships, technology and social networks can push this theory to its limits. Although technology has revolutionized how we connect with others, it cannot replace the personal touch of face-to-face interaction. Effort, communication, and a genuine interest in others are still crucial in building and maintaining relationships. Nevertheless, technology provides us with tools to easily connect and interact with people worldwide, streamline keeping relationships, and expand our network.

LinkedIn's Intero Advisory (LinkedIn) suggests that the more you truly know and understand the people in your network, the higher the likelihood of mutually beneficial interactions. To this end, LinkedIn recommends breaking down your connections into three categories:

- 80% should be people who are directly connected to your business, such as partners, clients, vendors, and colleagues. These individuals can provide valuable insights, resources, and opportunities for growth.
- 15% should be people you may not know yet but plan to actively pursue in the future. These could be potential partners, clients, or collaborators.
- 5% should be family and friends. These connections are essential for maintaining a healthy balance between personal and professional life.

It's worth noting that these percentages are suggested figures, and the actual breakdown you choose to follow will depend on your specific networking strategies. By regularly conducting a purge and aligning your connections with your goals, you can improve the quality and effectiveness of your network.

Time to Organize

Once you know that you have the right names on the list, you need a system to ensure that you can easily access them when the need arises. Keeping track of your professional contacts can be daunting, especially as your network grows. However, organizing your contacts is crucial for effectively leveraging your network and staying connected with the people who can help you achieve your goals. This chapter will discuss different strategies for organizing your contacts and how to manage your professional network effectively. From creating a contact database to using tools like LinkedIn and business cards, we will explore the best ways to stay organized and make the most of your professional connections.

Group People into Circles

We keep track of numerous names and groups—we have one for our business, social life, hobbies, family, and church. Managing so many can sometimes make us feel like we must include them all. However, we can determine if a connection is still relevant by categorizing them.

An online Customer Relationship Management (CRM) system simplifies the process of maintaining connections by making it easy to locate a connection. Using a CRM dedicated to networking ensures that names are correctly grouped, which helps prevent relevant connections from being lost.

Organizing the people we interact and connect with can help us feel less overwhelmed. When we have a visual representation of our network, we can stop worrying if we have the right people in our various groups and ease our stress. Grouping people in circles is one of the best ways to categorize and organize them. We already use the phrase "inner circle" to refer to a close group of people.

According to our research, the most commonly created circles are: Family, Friends, Leads, Clients, Work, Church, Neighbors, College/University, and Services. These can serve as a starting point for grouping your growing network of connections. You can use circle names to refer to each group and tie circles to various stages of a process model or relationship status.

For instance, you can have several circles bound by the sales cycle, such as lead, prospect, interested, client, etc. You can manage and work with individuals differently at each stage depending on which circle they are in. Another example is moving people through a relationship success set of circles (Level 1 through 4). People you've just met become Level one and are stored in the "Level 1" circle. As you develop a relationship, you can move that person from one level to the next, and each new corresponding circle. You might have different activities and exercises to engage with people at various levels.

You can also involve others in managing your circles. For instance, they can help you decide who should receive Christmas cards and birthday notes in the Level 1 circle, given the financial and time constraints and the large number of people in this circle. In contrast, those in the Level 4 circle may receive more personalized and sentimental expressions of gratitude, such as gift baskets.

Organizing your network into unique circles isn't just about efficiency; it's about stewardship. It's how we ensure we have the bandwidth, resources, and genuine intention to contribute to the lives of those around us. Reflecting on Philippians 2:3-4, we're reminded that this approach is not driven by selfish ambitions or a desire for reward. Instead, it's grounded in a humble commitment to prioritize the well-being and success of others above our own. "Do nothing out of selfish ambition or vain conceit. Rather, in humility value others above yourselves, not looking to your own interests but each of you to the interests of the others." This scripture underscores the essence of meaningful networking—it's about elevating those around us, recognizing that our greatest achievements come not from our individual efforts but from our ability to uplift one another.

Manage Your Network through Levels

Categorizing one's network into "levels" can be a useful way to develop habits for building and maintaining relationships. The levels are typically based on the depth and frequency of positive interactions with each person. For example, Level 0 might include contact data only, while Level 1 might represent a single positive interaction with someone. Level 2 might represent multiple positive interactions, and Level 3 might indicate a relationship in which you and the other person regularly serve each other in some way. Finally, Level 4 might indicate a relationship in which you feel a strong sense of trust and loyalty, such that you would be willing to pick the other person up from the airport in the middle of the night (Stewart, 2016).

The process of categorizing your network into levels is a useful system that can help you build deeper, more meaningful relationships with the people in your life. As stated previously, Dunbar's theory holds that we can only manage around 150 relationships at any one time, but you can nurture and maintain rewarding and fulfilling relationships with even more people by using the right approach and a bit of organization.

To get started, begin by categorizing your contacts into the different Levels, such as Level 0, Level 1, Level 2, Level 3, and Level 4. Each level represents the depth and frequency of positive interactions you have with a person, and you can develop habits to move people through the levels. For instance, you might set a goal to have at least one positive interaction each week with someone in your Level 0 or Level 1 category, such as sending them a friendly email or offering your help.

A great way to have a meaningful catch up or "touch" with someone in your network is to find articles that relate to their interests and email them with a simple note of "I read this and thought about you." This small gesture shows that you have been thinking about the person and their interests, opens up an opportunity for discussion, and helps move someone up to the next level in your network.

To cultivate relationships at Level 3 or Level 4, invest more time and effort into building trust and showing your willingness to serve the other person. Regular check-ins, offering your help with important tasks or projects, and finding ways to express your gratitude and appreciation for the other person are some ways to achieve this. Although these relationships are valuable and rewarding, they require more effort to maintain. While the average person can maintain about 150 relationships at a time, you may only be able to maintain about 30 relationships at Level 4 due to the amount of time and effort required.

Categorizing your network into levels can help you focus your efforts and energy on building deeper, more meaningful relationships with the people in your life. By consistently engaging in positive interactions and investing time and effort into building trust, you can move people through the Levels and cultivate valuable relationships that bring fulfillment and joy into your life. The key is to approach your relationships with intention, authenticity, and generosity. By doing so, you can create a network of supportive and meaningful relationships that can enhance your personal and professional life.

Maintaining Invaluable Relationships with Valuable Information

To build and maintain strong relationships, it is important to gather and store specific types of data. This data can be used to understand the needs and interests of your contacts and communicate with them in a personalized and meaningful way. The following sections contain the fundamental elements you may want to capture about your connections.

Contact Information: Basic contact information such as name, email address, and phone number is essential for keeping in touch with your contacts. It is important to keep this information up-to-date and accurate.

Demographic Data: Demographic data such as age, gender, occupation, and location can segment your contacts and tailor your outreach to their specific interests and needs. For example, you could search and mass-email all your left-handed contacts, celebrating them on August 13th.

Interaction Data: Tracking interaction data, such as emails, phone calls, and meetings, can provide valuable insight into the level of engagement and interest of your contacts. By keeping a record of these interactions, you can easily pick up where you left off in your conversations and avoid covering ground that you've already discussed. This helps you to maintain a better understanding of your relationship with each contact and enables you to build on previous discussions for more productive and efficient communication in the future.

Interests and Needs: Understanding the interests and needs of your contacts can help you tailor your communication and offerings to better meet their needs. This can include gathering information about their industry, job role, or specific interests. Having this level of detail on your network allows you to serve as a matchmaker, superconnector, and the person who makes introductions.

Communication Preferences: Knowing the preferred method of communication for your contacts can help you effectively reach them. Examples of this include whether they prefer email, text, phone, or in-person communication.

Relationship History: Keeping a record of the history of your relationship with a contact can help you understand the context of your interactions and anticipate their needs. (see the "Level Up" section regarding how to incorporate a process model in your networking).

By gathering and storing this data, you will be better equipped to build and maintain strong relationships. It's crucial to ensure that the data is kept secure and compliant with GDPR, CCPA, and other regulations where applicable. It's also important to be transparent about what data you collect, why you collect it, and who you share it with. For reference, General Data Protection Regulation (GDPR), is a regulation by the European Union on data protection and privacy for all individuals within the EU and the European Economic Area (EEA). It came into effect on May 25, 2018, and aims to protect the privacy and personal data of EU citizens. CCPA stands for California Consumer Privacy Act, which is a state-level privacy law in California that was passed in 2018 and became effective on January 1, 2020. The CCPA grants California consumers certain rights regarding their personal information and requires businesses that collect such information to provide specific disclosures and comply with certain rules and regulations. The CCPA is often regarded as the most comprehensive state-level data privacy law in the United States.

As you continue to gather and store data, regularly review, and update it to ensure that it is accurate and relevant. This will help you stay connected with your contacts and build long-lasting, meaningful relationships. By reviewing the relevant data about a person, you can strengthen your memory of important facts and details about them. This makes it easier to be responsive to their needs and demonstrates that you care about their interests and goals. Taking the time to review this information shows that you value your relationship with them and can help you build stronger connections.

The Power of the Catch-Up

The ability to follow up is a valuable skill that can make a significant impact on your networking success. When we go the extra mile and follow up, people remember us. We become a memorable face among a sea of forgettable names. The following are several ways to make your follow-up efforts more effective and leave a lasting impression.

Creating a Reconnection Schedule

When you have an extensive network, it's easy to get overwhelmed and lose track of who to follow up with. To prevent this, consider creating a reconnection schedule for each of your connections. This will help you manage your connections in a more systematic way and ensure that you stay in touch with everyone who matters. An online Customer Relationship Management (CRM) system can be especially helpful for organizing your connections and assigning specific dates for follow-ups. By using a CRM to keep track of your reconnection schedule, you can easily manage your network and maintain important relationships without feeling overwhelmed.

If you can connect with just five people daily, you will have 150 new meaningful connections by the end of 30 days. This may only be a fraction of your total LinkedIn connections, but that number, using the concept introduced in the first chapter that discussed Kevin Bacon and the Six Degrees of Separation, can significantly expand your network.

Setting Reminders for Reaching Out

When you connect with someone who receives a lot of messages, it's important to stand out and avoid being seen as just another sales pitch. To be successful in your messaging, it's crucial to know when to reach out. Take the time to learn about significant events in their life, such as upcoming birthdays, work anniversaries, or their participation in an event. You can also find common ground by celebrating relatable annual traditions like National Cupcake Day. By doing this, you can personalize your outreach and show that you care about their interests and achievements. This can help you to build a stronger connection and stand out in their busy inbox. Sending your message at the right time, with the right content, can be a game-changer. It shows that you care about their success and have taken the time to research and plan your outreach.

Sending a Personal Text Message

After receiving a business card at an event, consider setting a reminder to reintroduce yourself via a text message. Texting is a more informal way to connect, which allows the recipient to relax and not feel like you're just trying to make a sale. By using a personal tone and mentioning a previous conversation or shared interest, you can make a strong impression and stand out from the crowd. A helpful trick is to take a photo of the person's business card and attach it to their profile in your CRM. This way, you can easily access their contact information, and you can dispose of the physical card once it's no longer needed.

Sending a Non-Salesy Email

Sending an email is a great way to reconnect with potential business partners or investors. It is a formal and respectful way to initiate contact, and using a CRM can help you keep track of your email conversations to ensure they run smoothly and are timely. You can consider sharing the latest industry news and offering tips on how it can help grow their business as possible topics. This can pique their curiosity and lead to future opportunities and collaborations. Don't be surprised if they become interested in your expertise in their field, as this can further strengthen your relationship and foster more meaningful connections.

Making a Phone Call

Making random phone calls to professional connections is not the best way to create a solid business relationship. Still, making a call to close connections can mean the world to them. Special events like birthdays, anniversaries, or career milestones are occasions to call and demonstrate your care and support.

Writing a Letter

Nothing beats a handwritten letter, especially when it is genuine and written with the intent to help. Even the image of taking the time to write your thoughts speaks volumes. You can write a letter to share your appreciation for a connection, congratulate them on a recent achievement, or provide them with valuable information and resources.

CHAPTER 8

Bringing People Together

People are crucial to our success story. It is almost impossible to say, "I have achieved everything on my own." Throughout our journey, strangers, acquaintances, and friends have and will continue to contribute to our personal successes. The saying holds true—we need others to thrive.

Networking Groups

The sale of my first company came about from a casual lunch. Our company had more partners than employees, which is a testament to the importance of partnerships in growth. During one regular partner lunch, the conversation turned to the future of our two companies. Our partner was a multibillion-dollar company. They commented on how sometimes partnering with such a large company can be challenging, to which I responded, "Why not just buy us?" That question was met with a small laugh and the response, "Let's do it." A year later, they acquired us—all because of a networking lunch that I wasn't excited to attend. I learned a valuable lesson—no matter how reluctant you may be to socialize or attend an event, go, as it may be the open door you're hoping for.

Adam Grant, a researcher at the Wharton School of Business, conducted a study on workplace dynamics and found that the greatest untapped source of motivation is a sense of service to others. By focusing on how our work contributes to others' lives, we can become more productive and motivated than if we were solely focused on helping ourselves (Grant, 2013)

To make networking work for you, start by providing value to others. Share your expertise, offer to help, and be open to learning from others. This will set you apart from the crowd and establish you as a valuable member of the community.

Another key to successful networking is to make sales a secondary agenda. Instead of focusing on closing deals, focus on building genuine connections with others. By making people feel valued and appreciated, you'll create deeper, more meaningful relationships that can lead to new opportunities down the road.

Another way to make networking work for you is by supporting a cause or starting your own networking group. Joining or starting a group that is focused on a specific cause or industry can provide a natural way to connect with others who share your interests and passions. Additionally, by starting your own group, you can tailor the group to your specific needs and interests, and streamline your networking efforts.

Networking is a crucial component of building connections and achieving success. However, to truly benefit from it, one must shift their focus from self-promotion to giving back, providing value, and fostering genuine connections with others. By supporting a cause, creating a community, or prioritizing relationship-building over sales, you can unlock the full potential of networking and achieve greater heights of success.

Networking Success Story #4

The Happiest Place on Earth

Jeremy was not a fan of networking events. The thought of walking into a room full of strangers and trying to make small talk made him break out in a cold sweat. So, when he received an invitation to a networking lunch, he immediately wanted to decline. However, his mentor convinced him that it was an opportunity he couldn't afford to miss.

Despite his mentor's convincing, Jeremy arrived at the restaurant feeling nervous and out of place. He didn't know anyone, and everyone else seemed to be chatting and laughing with one another. But, as he made his way to the table, he remembered his mentor's words: "Remember to listen more than you talk, ask questions, and follow up."

Jeremy took a deep breath and approached the group. He found himself sitting next to a man named Dave who worked at Disneyland, his lifelong dream job. Jeremy couldn't believe his luck. He started off the conversation by asking Dave about his job and showed genuine interest in what he had to say. They talked about the different attractions and what it was like to work at the Happiest Place on Earth.

By the end of the lunch, Jeremy was so engrossed in their conversation that he almost forgot about the rest of the group. When lunch was over, Jeremy made sure to get Dave's business card and followed up with him the next day. They continued to keep in touch, and eventually, Dave offered Jeremy a job at Disneyland.

Jeremy couldn't believe his luck. He never thought that a simple networking lunch would lead him to his lifelong goal. He was grateful for the advice he received from his mentor and how it helped him make the most of this opportunity. From that day on, Jeremy made sure to always attend networking events and put his best foot forward. He learned that by showing genuine interest in others, remembering important details, and following up, he could open doors to life's successes.

Networking Groups to Follow

Networking is an essential aspect of building a successful business, and there are many different types of networking groups available to help people connect with others in their industry. Whether you're looking for an industry-specific group, a group focused on a specific demographic, or a group based on location or a cause, there's a networking group that can offer you valuable support and connections.

Industry-specific groups, such as finance, marketing, or technology, provide valuable opportunities to connect with others in your field and learn about the latest trends and best practices. Demographic-specific groups, such as women in business or young entrepreneurs, offer support and resources tailored to the unique challenges and opportunities that members of that group may face. Regional or city-based groups offer the opportunity to connect with other business owners and entrepreneurs in the same area, and groups focused on causes or social issues provide a platform for business people who are passionate about a specific cause and want to make a positive impact in their community.

To help you get started, here are a few popular and successful networking groups to consider: the Women in Business network, Business Networking International, the Young Entrepreneurs Council, and the American Marketing Association.

- Women in Business: A networking group dedicated to female entrepreneurs that offers valuable support and connections in various fields such as STEM and arts and crafts.

- Business Networking International (BNI): A referral-based organization that is considered as the world's largest, it is a community of business owners who support one another through referrals. In 2018, it was recorded that the referrals made within the group generated up to $14 billion in income.

- Young Entrepreneurs Council: An invitation-only, fee-based organization that is dedicated to entrepreneurs who are still paving their way in business and are 45 years old and below.

- American Marketing Association: A networking group dedicated to marketers of all levels that provides access to marketing best practices and support to connect businesses with people.

Each of these groups offers unique opportunities to connect with people in your field and grow your business. Whether you're looking to expand your professional network, gain new insights and knowledge, or make meaningful connections, these groups can help you achieve your goals.

Networking Groups and the Enriching Power They Hold

In ancient India, a parable was told of an elephant and a group of blind men. Each man was led to a different part of the elephant's body and was asked to describe what they felt. The man who touched the trunk declared it to be a snake, while the man who touched the ear insisted it was a fan. Others who touched the sides of the elephant perceived it to be a wall.

Are we not all like those blind men? We all have our own ideas and beliefs that we hold onto tightly, without truly knowing if they are accurate or not.

Imagine if we were to live our lives holding onto the belief that nothing is ever truly true and that nothing can bring us success except for what we already know. How limiting and unfulfilling that would be.

One of the best ways to expand our horizons is by broadening our network. The people in our networks can enrich our knowledge and help us to grow our ideas. Through networking, we can consciously put aside the things that hinder our view and begin to see the bigger picture, one that allows us to understand and appreciate more.

Starting Your Own Networking Group

"We cannot achieve greatness alone. We need others to lift us up, to inspire us, and to help us become the best version of ourselves."
—SIMON SINEK

Building a strong network of peers can be instrumental to your personal and professional growth. Mastermind and networking groups are an excellent way to build and maintain these connections. These groups offer a supportive and collaborative environment where individuals can share knowledge, expertise, and resources. Starting a mastermind or networking group requires careful planning and execution. Here are some steps to follow:

Step 1

Define the Purpose and Goals of Your Group

Before you start inviting people, you must clearly define the purpose and goals of your group. What is the focus of the group? Who is your target audience? What do you want to achieve? Some common goals of mastermind and networking groups are professional development, business growth, and socializing. Knowing the answers to these questions will help you attract the right people and ensure that your groups activities are aligned with your goals.

Step 2

Determine the Group Size and Structure

The size of your group will depend on your goals and the nature of your activities. The optimal size for a mastermind group is typically between 4 and 8 people. Networking groups can be larger. You should also decide on the structure of your group, such as the frequency of meetings, the format of the sessions, and the topics to be discussed.

Step 3

Invite

Once you have a clear purpose, goals, and structure in place, you can start inviting potential members. Reach out to people in your professional and personal networks, and consider using social media, professional organizations, and other online platforms to find potential members. You can also ask your existing members to refer people they know who would be a good fit.

Step 4

Facilitate the First Meeting

The first meeting is crucial for setting the tone of the group and establishing expectations. It's important to make sure that everyone has a chance to introduce themselves and get to know each other. You should also take the opportunity to clarify the group's purpose and goals and set the agenda for future meetings. It is a good idea to assign a facilitator for each meeting, who will be responsible for ensuring that the discussion stays on topic and that everyone has a chance to participate.

Step 5

Maintain Momentum

To keep the group engaged and motivated, it's essential to maintain momentum. Set a regular meeting schedule and send out reminders to members in advance of each meeting. It's also a good idea to rotate the meeting location and the facilitator for each session. Consider setting up a communication channel outside of meetings, such as a group chat or email list, to facilitate ongoing discussions and information sharing.

Step 6

Evaluate and Adjust as Necessary

As the group evolves, it's important to evaluate its effectiveness and adjust as necessary. You should regularly solicit feedback from members, and use this feedback to refine the group's purpose, goals, and activities. It's also important to be open to new members and ideas, as this will keep the group dynamic and relevant.

Starting a mastermind or networking group takes time and effort, but the benefits can be immense. By creating a supportive and collaborative environment, you can develop meaningful relationships, gain new insights and perspectives, and accelerate your personal and professional growth.

The Opportunity to Network Is Everywhere!

Networking is not only about trading information, but also serves as an avenue to create long-term relationships with mutual benefits. —FORBES

Networking is not just about attending big events and mingling with people in the business world. It's about making connections, building relationships, and creating opportunities for yourself and others. The beauty of networking is that the opportunities to do so are everywhere. From striking up a conversation with a stranger in line, to greeting your neighbor on their first day in their new home, to visiting a newly opened business and chatting with its owners, the opportunities are endless.

The power of a simple greeting can never be underestimated. Saying "Hi" to someone new can lead to surprising connections, as you may find out that you have common friends. By making personalized, sincere messages for your online connections, you can leave a lasting impression and create meaningful relationships.

The key to successful networking is to see beyond the stress of making connections and embrace the fun and excitement that comes with building meaningful relationships. Whether you're just starting out or have been networking for years, remember that the chance to network is everywhere. So, take advantage of every opportunity that comes your way and make each connection matter.

As we reflect on the journey of networking and the countless opportunities it presents, let us be reminded of the wisdom found in Ecclesiastes 4:9-10: "Two are better than one; because they have a good reward for their labor. For if they fall, the one will lift up his fellow: but woe to him that is alone when he falleth; for he hath not another to help him up." This scripture encapsulates the essence of networking—it's about more than just building a web of contacts. It's about creating a community of support, where we can lift each other up, celebrate successes, and offer a helping hand during challenges. It reminds us that in the fabric of human connection, every strand is intertwined, and together, we are stronger and more capable of achieving our goals.

It's my greatest hope that through this book, you have learned to appreciate the power of networking and discover the opportunities that are waiting for you, right at your fingertips. Let us move forward with the understanding that our connections are not just pathways to personal and professional growth but also avenues for contributing to the well-being and success of others. In every greeting, conversation, and interaction, lies the potential for profound impact. May we all strive to be a beacon of support and kindness in our networks, illuminating the way for others as we journey together towards our goals.

GLOSSARY

Association: A group of individuals or organizations that share a common interest or goal, often used as a networking tool to connect with like-minded individuals.

Brand identity: The visual and verbal representation of a brand, including its name, logo, messaging, and overall image.

Business card: A physical card that contains one's contact information, often exchanged during professional networking events.

Business networking: The act of establishing and maintaining professional relationships with other businesses and organizations.

Cold call: An unsolicited phone call made to a potential contact with whom the caller has no prior relationship, typically used as a means of networking or making a business pitch.

Cold email: An unsolicited email sent to a recipient with whom the sender has no prior relationship, typically used as a means of networking or making a business pitch.

Community outreach: The act of connecting with and supporting the local community through volunteer work, sponsorships, and other forms of engagement.

Contacts: Individuals or groups that one can connect with for professional reasons.

Digital footprint: The trail of information that is left behind when one uses the internet or other digital media, including social media activity and online search history.

Elevator pitch: A concise, well-crafted description of oneself or one's business that can be delivered in the time it takes to ride an elevator.

Elevator speech: A brief and persuasive speech used to introduce oneself or a business to a potential contact, typically delivered in a networking or social setting.

Follow-up: The act of reaching out to contacts after an initial meeting or interaction in order to maintain the relationship and further the conversation.

Follow-up email: An email sent after an initial meeting or conversation with a contact to further the relationship and move the conversation forward.

Group networking: Networking within a group of like-minded individuals with a shared interest or goal.

Industry: A specific field or sector of the economy, such as healthcare, finance, or technology.

Informational interview: A meeting between an individual and someone in their desired field or industry, typically for the purpose of gathering information and making connections.

Job search networking: The act of connecting with potential employers or recruiters through networking as a means of finding job opportunities.

LinkedIn: A social media platform designed for professional networking, job searching, and career development.

Mastermind group: A group of individuals who meet regularly to provide support, feedback, and advice to one another in a specific field or industry.

Mentor: A more experienced individual who provides guidance, advice, and support to a less experienced individual.

Network referral: A recommendation from a contact for someone to join a professional network or organization.

Networking: The act of establishing and maintaining professional relationships with individuals and groups for the purpose of mutual benefit.

Networking event: A professional event or gathering designed for the purpose of meeting and connecting with new contacts.

Networking skills: The ability to effectively communicate, connect, and build relationships with others for the purpose of advancing one's career or business.

Networking strategy: A well-planned and intentional approach to networking that is designed to achieve specific professional goals.

Niche: A specialized area or segment of an industry or market.

Online networking: The use of online tools and platforms to connect with potential contacts, build relationships, and further one's career or business.

Personal branding: The act of defining and presenting oneself in a unique and positive way to stand out and make a lasting impression on potential contacts.

Personal mission statement: A statement that outlines one's core values, goals, and purpose in life or career.

Professional associations: Groups of professionals who share a common interest or field and collaborate to advance their profession through networking, training, and other activities.

Professional development: The process of continuously developing and enhancing one's skills, knowledge, and expertise to further one's career.

Referral: The act of recommending someone for a job or business opportunity.

Small talk: Light, casual conversation used to break the ice and establish rapport with new acquaintances.

Social media: Online platforms and tools used to share information, connect with others, and build networks.

Target market: A specific group of consumers or businesses that a product or service is intended to reach and serve.

Value proposition: A statement that outlines the unique value or benefit that one can offer to potential contacts, clients, or employers. A strong value proposition can help one stand out from the competition and make a strong impression on others.

Warm introduction: A connection made between two people through a mutual acquaintance, which can be an effective way to establish rapport and build trust.

Word-of-mouth: An informal means of communication in which people share information or opinions about a product, service, or person through personal conversations or social media.

APPENDIX: STATISTICS

According to a LinkedIn survey, 85% of all jobs are filled through networking. (Source: LinkedIn) LinkedIn. LinkedIn Official Blog. 19 May 2015, https://blog.linkedin.com/2015/05/19/how-job-seekers-are-using-linkedin-to-get-hired-today.

Networking can increase your salary by up to 15%. (Source: Harvard Business Review)Casciaro, Tiziana, and Miguel Sousa Lobo. How to Network Effectively. Harvard Business Review, vol. 87, no. 12, Dec. 2009, pp. 132-139.

Networking can increase your salary by up to 15%. (Source: Harvard Business Review) Casciaro, Tiziana, and Miguel Sousa Lobo. How to Network Effectively. Harvard Business Review, vol. 87, no. 12, Dec. 2009, pp. 132-139.

Approximately 70% of jobs are never advertised publicly, and are instead filled through referrals or networking. (Source: U.S. Bureau of Labor Statistics)U.S. Bureau of Labor Statistics. Career Guide to Industries, 2010-11 Edition: Job Search Methods and Tools. Jan. 2010, https://www.bls.gov/careeroutlook/2010/winter/art01.pdf.

People who network regularly are more likely to receive job offers and advance in their careers. (Source: Forbes)Weissbourd, Beth K. Why Networking Is The Most Important Skill You Can Have. Forbes, 12 Mar. 2015, https://www.forbes.com/sites/learnvest/2015/03/12/why-networking-is-the-most-important-skill-you-can-have/#6b3ed3c94d9d.

In a study of more than 4,000 professionals, those who had larger professional networks were more likely to be promoted and have higher job satisfaction.

Cross, Rob, et al. The Benefits of Reciprocity in Work Relationships. Harvard Business Review, vol. 87, no. 1/2, Jan.-Feb. 2009, pp. 104-111.

40% of people say that they have gotten a job through a personal connection. (Source: Glassdoor)Glassdoor. 50 HR and Recruiting Stats for 2019. 11 Dec. 2018, https://www.glassdoor.com/blog/50-hr-recruiting-stats-2019/.

According to a study by the Adler Group, executives with larger networks earn on average 22% more than those with smaller networks. (Source: The Muse)Cenedella, Kathryn. Your Career Is Only as Strong as Your Network: The Adler Group Study. The Muse, 24 Feb. 2015, https://www.themuse.com/advice/your-career-is-only-as-strong-as-your-network-the-adler-group-study.

People who build and maintain a diverse network are more likely to have innovative ideas and solve problems more effectively. (Source: Scientific American)Galinsky, Adam D., et al. How Diversity Makes Us Smarter. Scientific American, Oct. 2017, pp. 42-47.

LinkedIn is the most popular social media platform for professional networking, with over 760 million users worldwide. (Source: LinkedIn) LinkedIn. About LinkedIn. *https://about.linkedin.com/*.

QUOTES

You can make more friends in two months by becoming interested in other people than you can in two years by trying to get other people interested in you.

Talk to someone about themselves and they listen for hours.

Whenever you go out-of-doors, Draw the chin in, carry the crown of the head high, and fill the lungs to the utmost; drink in the sunshine; greet your friends with a smile; and put your soul into every handclasp.

Talk in terms of other people's interests.

To be interesting, be interested.

Carnegie, Dale. How to Win Friends and
Influence People. Simon and Schuster, 1981.

As Dale Carnegie once said, "A person's name is, to that person, the sweetest, most important sound in any language" (Carnegie, 1936). Remembering someone's name shows that you're invested in building a relationship with them, and that small act of kindness can go a long way.

About 15 percent of one's financial success is due to one's technical knowledge and about 85 percent is due to skill in human engineering—to personality and the ability to lead people.

Carnegie, Dale. How to Win Friends and
Influence People. Simon and Schuster, 1981.

Relationships are hard. But think about it, it's the one thing we all want. To love and be loved. And the one thing that holds us back is just how hard relationships are.

Sinek, Simon. Start with Why: How Great Leaders
Inspire Everyone to Take Action. Penguin, 2011.

CITATIONS

Ambady, Nalini, and Robert Rosenthal. "Thin slices of expressive behavior as predictors of interpersonal consequences: A meta-analysis." Psychological Bulletin, vol. 111, no. 2, 1992, pp. 256-274.

Carnegie, Dale. "Six ways to make people like you." How to Win Friends and Influence People, Simon & Schuster, 1936, p. 49.

"Dunbar's number." ScienceDirect, Elsevier BV, 2022, www.sciencedirect.com/topics/computer-science/dunbars-number.

Dyer, Jeff, et al. The Innovator's DNA: Mastering the Five Skills of Disruptive Innovators. Harvard Business Review Press, 2011.

Fern, Sarah. "Skills that Matter: Why Empathy and Human Connection are on the Rise." The HR Director, 14 Sept. 2021, https://www.thehrdirector.com/features/the-workplace/skills-that-matter-why-empathy-and-human-connection-are-on-the-rise/.

Grant, Adam M. Give and Take: A Revolutionary Approach to Success. Viking, 2013.

Heunis, Lizel. "Securing Gainful Employment Is Easier Than You Think: Part 1." LinkedIn, 27 Jan. 2022, https://www.linkedin.com/pulse/securing-gainful-employment-easier-than-you-think-part-lizel-heunis-1f/.

Horn, Sam. "The Art of Being Interesting: TEDxUCLA." YouTube, uploaded by TEDx Talks, 28 Nov. 2016, https://www.youtube.com/watch?v=FD247KyXr6o.

Intero Advisory. "About Intero Advisory." LinkedIn, LinkedIn Corporation, 2022, www.linkedin.com/company/intero-advisory/about/.

Kondo, Marie. The Life-Changing Magic of Tidying Up: The Japanese Art of Decluttering and Organizing. Translated by Cathy Hirano, Ten Speed Press, 2014.

Sinek, Simon. Together Is Better: A Little Book of Inspiration. Penguin Random House, 2016.

Smith, J. "The Six Degrees of Kevin Bacon: Exploring Network Theory Through Popular Culture." Journal of Popular Culture, vol. 53, no. 3, 2020, pp. 713-728, doi: 10.1111/jpcu.12931.

Statistic Brain Research Institute. "Business Card Statistics." Statistic Brain, 18 Jan. 2018, https://www.statisticbrain.com/business-card-statistics/.

Stewart, Jared. The City of Influence: A Business Tale. 2016.

"The Rise of Superconnectors." Forbes, 20 Feb. 2014, https://www.forbes.com/sites/stevedenning/2014/02/20/the-rise-of-superconnectors/?sh=3e390ce63272.

The Walt Disney Company. (2024). About. Retrieved February 1, 2024, from https://thewaltdisneycompany.com/about/

We Are Social, DataReportal, and Meltwater. "Digital 2023: Global Overview Report." Digital 2023: Global Overview Report, Jan. 2023, p. 182

ACKNOWLEDGEMENTS

This book is a testament to the power of faith, family, and community. Dana, my eternal companion, your love and support have been a constant reminder of God's grace in my life. Through every challenge, your unwavering faith has strengthened mine.

Emma and Seth, my precious children, your patience with an often-distracted dad has been a lesson in Christ-like love.

To my students, especially Chase Labrum and Devin Rockwood, I'm grateful for the way you've exemplified the principle of lifelong learning. Your dedication and insights have been instrumental in bringing this work to fruition, showing how we can lift and strengthen one another.

www.ingramcontent.com/pod-product-compliance
Lightning Source LLC
Chambersburg PA
CBHW070901280326
41934CB00008B/1540